Jane Eyre

B Y

Charlotte Brontë

EDITED BY
Philip Page and Marilyn Pettit

ILLUSTRATED BY
Philip Page

Published in association with

Hodder & Stoughton

A MEMBER OF THE HODDER HEADLINE

Orders: please contact Bookpoint Ltd, 130 Milton Park, Abingdon, Oxon OX14 4SB.
Telephone: (44) 01235 827720, fax: (44) 01235 400454. Lines are open from 9.00–6.00,
Monday to Saturday, with a 24 hour message answering service. You can also order
through our website www.hodderheadline.co.uk

British Library Cataloguing in Publication Data
A catalogue record for this title is available from the British Library

ISBN 0 340 87160 1

First Published 2003
Impression number   10 9 8 7 6 5 4 3 2 1
Year   2009 2008 2007 2006 2005 2004 2003

Cover illustration by Dave Smith.
Typeset by Fakenham Photosetting Ltd, Norfolk.
Printed in Great Britain for Hodder & Stoughton Educational, a division of Hodder
Headline, 338 Euston Road, London NW1 3BH by J.W. Arrowsmith, Bristol.

Contents

About the story

Charlotte Brontë wrote poetry and a number of novels. Many people say that *Jane Eyre* is her most famous novel.

It was published in 1847 and has been filmed many times. It has even been made into a musical!

Any novel that has a person's name as its title makes the reader want to know something about that character. Some people say that Jane Eyre is a romantic heroine; others think that she is a strong-willed woman who showed the readers of the time that women could be independent and passionate. Some readers think that the novel is written as an autobiography, since the story was written by Jane and in it she tells us about her life. Other people think that it is also a love story, or that it is an 'education novel', showing how a person grows from childhood into adulthood.

Once you have finished your reading, you can make up your own mind about Jane and the novel.

Cast of characters

Jane Eyre

age 10   age 18   age 28

At Gateshead Hall

Mrs Reed
Jane's aunt.

John Reed
Her son.

Bessie
A servant.

Mr Lloyd
A local chemist.

At Lowood School

Mr Brocklehurst
The man in charge
of the school.

Miss Temple Miss Scatcherd
Teachers.

Helen Burns
Jane's friend.

At Thornfield Hall

Edward Rochester
The master of
Thornfield Hall.

Mrs Fairfax
The housekeeper.

Grace Poole   **Leah**
Servants.

Adèle Varens
Mr Rochester's ward.

Blanche Ingram
Visitors to Thornfield Hall.

Richard Mason

Bertha Mason
Richard's sister.

Mr Briggs
A solicitor.

Mr Wood
A clergyman.

At Moor House

St John Rivers   **Diana Rivers**
A clergyman.   His sister.

At Ferndean Manor

Mary   **John**
Servants.

Jane has a very unhappy life, living with her aunt and cousins.

There was no possibility of taking a walk that day. I was glad: I never liked long walks.

Eliza, John, and Georgiana were round their mama.

What does Bessie say I have done?

Jane, until you can speak pleasantly, remain silent.

A small breakfast-room **adjoined** the drawing room: I slipped in there, into the window-seat.

I was happy.

Where is she?

In the window-seat.

What do you want?

Say 'what do you want, Master Reed'.

I want you to come here.

He struck suddenly and strongly.

I felt him grasp my hair.

I don't know what I did with my hands, but he **bellowed** out aloud.

adjoined – was next to
bellowed – yelled

We were parted.

Take her away to the red-room, and lock her in there.

Hold her arms; she's like a mad cat.

You should try to be pleasant; but if you become rude, Missis will send you away.

This room was chill. My head ached and bled. I grew cold.

I rushed to the door and shook the lock.

Take me out!

She has screamed on purpose. I know her naughty tricks.

You will now stay here an hour longer.

Aunt, have pity!

Mrs Reed locked me in.

Luckily for Jane, a kind man suggests she goes away to school.

The next thing I remember is, waking up in my own bed. A gentleman sat in a chair, leaning over me. It was Mr Lloyd, an **apothecary**.

What made you ill?

She had a fall.

Nurse, you can go.

The fall did not make you ill; what did?

I am very unhappy. I have no father or mother, brothers or sisters.

Have you any relations besides Mrs Reed?

Aunt Reed said I might have some poor relations; a beggarly set.

Would you like to go to school?

I should indeed.

apothecary – chemist (used instead of a doctor)

Arrangements for Jane to leave are finally made.

It was the fifteenth of January, about nine o'clock in the morning. Bessie came running upstairs.

I was wanted in the breakfast-room.

Mrs Reed occupied her usual seat and introduced me.

This is the little girl.

Well, Jane Eyre, are you a good child?

I was silent.

Perhaps the less said on that subject the better, Mr Brocklehurst.

Mr Brocklehurst, this girl has not quite the character I could wish.

She shall be watched. I will speak to the teachers.

I may depend upon this child being a pupil at Lowood?

Madam, you may.

I will send her as soon as possible.

Mr Brocklehurst departed.

Go out of the room; return to the nursery.

I am glad you are no relation of mine. I will never call you aunt again.

I will never come to see you when I am grown up; and if any one asks me how you treated me, I will say with miserable cruelty.

How dare you.

How dare I? Because it is the *truth*.

Send me to school soon, for I hate to live here.

Jane goes to Lowood School where she has to get used to the hard daily routine.

On the morning of the 19th of January the coach drew up at the gates.

Take good care of her.

I remember little of the journey. We passed through several towns. We descended a valley, dark with wood. I dropped asleep.

The coach-door was open.

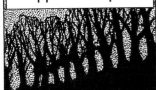

Is there a little girl called Jane Eyre here?

Rain, wind, and darkness filled the air.

We went up a broad pebbly path and were admitted at a door.

The child is very young to be sent alone. She had better be put to bed soon; she looks tired.

The night passed rapidly: a loud bell was ringing: the girls were up and dressing; day had not yet begun to dawn. I rose; and dressed shivering, and washed. There was one basin to six girls.

A distant bell tinkled. Business now began:

... reading the Bible ...

... breakfast: burnt porridge.

Lessons began; **repetitions** in history; writing and arithmetic. Each lesson was measured by the clock.

Dinner was potatoes and **rusty** meat.

After dinner, lessons continued till five o'clock.

After five we had another meal of a small mug of coffee, and half a slice of brown bread. Half an hour's **recreation**, then study, prayers, and bed.

Such was my first day at Lowood.

repetitions – repeating facts from memory
recreation – play, leisure

rusty – rancid, bad

8

Jane finds that life at Lowood can be cruel too, but she makes a new friend.

The next day the class stood round Miss Scatcherd's chair reading.

Burns, you dirty, disagreeable girl! You have never cleaned your nails this morning!

Burns made no answer.

Why does she not explain that she could neither clean her nails nor wash her face, as the water was frozen?

Burns left the class, and returned in half a minute, carrying a bundle of twigs tied together at one end.

Miss Scatcherd instantly and sharply inflicted on her neck a dozen strokes.

Not a feature of her face altered.

On the evening of the day on which I had seen Miss Scatcherd flog Burns, I made my way to one of the fire-places.

There, I found Burns.

What is your name besides Burns?

Helen.

You must wish to leave Lowood?

No: why should I? I was sent to Lowood to get an education.

But Miss Scatcherd is so cruel to you?

Cruel? Not at all! She is severe: she dislikes my faults.

If I were in your place, I should resist her; if she struck me with that rod, I should break it under her nose. I could not bear it.

It would be your duty to bear it, if you could not avoid it.

I heard her with wonder.

My first quarter at Lowood seemed an age. Our clothing was insufficient to protect us from the cold and the **scanty** supply of food was distressing.

One afternoon, I recognized Mr Brocklehurst with three other visitors.

My slate happened to slip from my hand.

Let the child who broke her slate, come forward!

Fetch that stool. Place the child upon it.

scanty – poor

Ladies, you all see this girl?

Who would think that the **Evil One** had found a servant in her? Be on your guard against her, avoid her. Teachers, you must watch her, punish her, for this girl is – a liar!

This I learned from the lady who adopted her. Let her stand on that stool, and let no one speak to her during the remainder of the day.

Five o'clock struck and all were gone. I sat down on the floor and wept. I wished to die. While sobbing out this wish, some one approached: Helen Burns.

Come, eat something.

Evil One – Devil

Why do you stay with a girl whom everybody believes to be a liar?

If all the world hated you, you would not be without friends.

I was silent: Helen had calmed me. Another person came in: Miss Temple.

I came to find you, Jane.

Have you cried your grief away?

I have been wrongly accused; everybody will think me wicked.

We shall think you what you prove yourself to be.

I told her the story of my sad childhood and mentioned Mr Lloyd.

I know Mr Lloyd; I shall write to him.

About a week **subsequently**, Miss Temple received his answer.

Miss Maria Temple, Superintendent, Lowood Institution

Miss Temple announced the charges alleged against Jane Eyre completely cleared.

I would not now have exchanged Lowood for **Gateshead** and its daily luxuries.

subsequently – after
Gateshead – Mrs Reed's house

13

Although Jane is now happier at Lowood, there are still times of sadness for her.

Where Lowood lay was the cradle of fog and bred **pestilence**. Forty-five out of the eighty girls lay ill at one time. Many went home to die; some died at the school.

How is Helen Burns?

Very poorly. She'll not be here long.

May I speak to her?

Oh, no, child!

Two hours later, I crept off. I found the door.

Helen! Are you awake? I could not sleep till I had spoken to you.

You came to bid me good-bye, then.

. . . you are just in time probably.

I feel as if I could sleep; but don't leave me, Jane.

No one shall take me away.

Her grave is in Brocklebridge churchyard; for fifteen years it was only covered by a grassy mound; but now a marble tablet marks the spot.

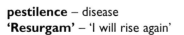

pestilence – disease
'Resurgam' – 'I will rise again'

The years pass. Jane learns a great deal and is successful, but she wants new adventures.

The school improved and I had an excellent education. I rose to be a teacher.

I have served here eight years; now all I want is a new place, in a new house, amongst new faces.

Those who want **situations** advertise.

A young lady **accustomed to tuition** is desirous of meeting with a situation in a private family where the children are under fourteen. She is qualified to teach English, French, Drawing, and Music. Address, J. E., Post-office . . .

I slipped the letter into the post-office. The week seemed long.

If J. E., who advertised last Thursday is in a position to give satisfactory references, a situation can be offered her where there is a little girl, under ten; the salary is thirty pounds **per annum**. Send references to Mrs Fairfax, Thornfield, near Millcote . . .

Are there any letters for J. E.?

Is there only one?

situations – jobs
accustomed to tuition – used to teaching
per annum – each year

Millcote was nearer London than the county where I now **resided**. I longed to go where there was life and movement; it would be a complete change.

A fortnight passed and I mounted the vehicle which was to bear me to new duties and a new life.

When the coach stopped, I looked round.

Is your name Eyre, Miss?

The roads were heavy, the night misty.

We slowly came upon the house. The front door was opened by a maidservant.

Will you walk this way, ma'am?

Mrs Fairfax was knitting. She got up and came forward to meet me.

How do you do, my dear? You must be cold, come to the fire.

I am so glad you are come.

resided – lived

Jane begins her job as governess at Thornfield Hall, but something is not quite right in this house!

That night I slept soundly. **I stepped over the threshold.** It was a fine autumn morning.

Out already? I see you are an early riser.

How do you like Thornfield? It is a pretty place; but I fear it will be getting out of order, unless Mr Rochester should come and reside here permanently.

Who is he?

The owner. I am only the housekeeper.

And the little girl – my pupil?

She is Mr Rochester's **ward**.

I stepped over the threshold – I went outside.
ward – child placed in the protection of a guardian.

Miss Adela. Come and speak to the lady who is to teach you.

After breakfast, Adèle and I withdrew to the library.

When the morning had advanced to noon, I allowed her to return to her nurse.

Mr Rochester's visits here are rare, and always unexpected. I keep the rooms in readiness.

Is he liked?

Oh yes. He is rather peculiar, but a very good master.

She proposed to show me over the rest of the house.

You have no ghost then?

None that I ever heard of.

While I paced on, the last sound I expected to hear, a laugh, struck my ears.

It was a curious laugh; **mirthless**.

Did you hear that?

Some of the servants very likely, perhaps Grace Poole.

Grace!

I should have been afraid.

The door opened and a servant came out.

Too much noise, Grace! Remember **directions**!

mirthless – without humour
directions – orders

Jane finally meets the master of Thornfield.

One afternoon in January, I walked a mile from Thornfield. I sat down on a stile.

I lingered till the sun went down. A horse was coming. I sat still to let it go by. The horse approached, on its back a rider.

He passed and they slipped on the ice.

Are you injured, sir?

Only a sprain.

Where do you come from?

Just below.

Whose house?

Mr Rochester's.

Do you know Mr Rochester?

No, I have never seen him.

You are—?

I am the governess

Ah, the governess! I had forgotten!

He sprang to his saddle and vanished.

I hurried on to the hall.

Mr Rochester is just arrived. Master has had an accident; his horse fell.

I went up stairs to take off my things.

Thornfield Hall had a master: I liked it better. Next day Mrs Fairfax came.

Mr Rochester would be glad if you would take tea with him this evening.

I was **summoned.**

Here is Miss Eyre, sir.

Let Miss Eyre be seated.

Who are your parents?

I have none.

Brocklehurst directs Lowood? You girls probably worshipped him.

No. I disliked Mr Brocklehurst. He is a harsh man. He starved us and he bored us.

Adele showed me some sketches, which she said were yours. Were you happy when you painted these pictures?

Yes.

It is nine o'clock. Good-night.

summoned – sent for

He is very **abrupt**.

He has family troubles.

I should have liked something clearer; but Mrs Fairfax wished me to drop the subject.

For several days I saw little of Mr Rochester. One day a message came that I and Adèle were to go downstairs to the dining-room. Mr Rochester had a smile on his lips.

Do you think me handsome?

No, sir.

Miss Eyre; you are not pretty any more than I am handsome.

It would please me to learn more of you – speak.

I don't think, sir, you have a right to command me, because you are older than I.

I don't understand you at all.

I rose.

Where are you going?

To put Adèle to bed. It has struck nine, sir.

abrupt – rude

23

It seems that Mr Rochester and Jane are becoming friends. Then, one night, an awful thing happens that brings them closer.

For some weeks, when he met me, he had a smile. I talked little, but I heard him **with relish**. I was happy with this new interest added to life.

And was Mr Rochester ugly in my eyes? No. He was proud, moody too, but I believed he was a man of excellent materials.

I was laid down in bed thinking.

Will he leave again? If he does, how joyless sunshine and fine days will seem!

I started wide awake. I rose listening. It seemed my door was touched.

Who is there?

Nothing answered. I was chilled with fear.

with relish – with enthusiasm

A **demoniac** laugh uttered at the very key-hole of my door.

I could see nothing.

Something moaned. Steps retreated. I opened the door.

I became aware of a strong smell of burning.

Mr Rochester's chamber.

Tongues of flame darted round the bed: the curtains were on fire.

Mr Rochester lay in deep sleep.

Wake! wake!

I **deluged** the bed, and succeeded in **extinguishing** the flames.

demoniac – devilish **deluged** – soaked **extinguishing** – putting out

Is there a flood?

No, but there has been a fire.

Who did it?

I briefly related the strange laugh I had heard.

Sit down. I must pay a visit to the third **story**. Don't move, or call any one.

A long time **elapsed** and then he re-entered.

I have found it all out.

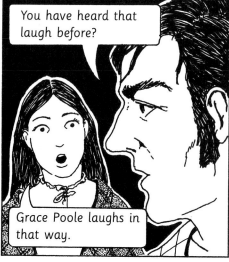

You have heard that laugh before?

Grace Poole laughs in that way.

Just so. Grace Poole.

Say nothing about it.

You have saved my life.

elapsed – passed
story – floor

26

Mr Rochester leaves for a few weeks. Jane realizes that she thinks a great deal of her master.

The morning passed. When **dusk closed** I listened for Mr Rochester. I wanted to ask him why he kept **her** wickedness a secret.

Is Mr Rochester gone anywhere?

The Leas; Mr Eshton's place. I believe there is quite a party there.

Do you expect him back to-night?

No, I should think he is very likely to stay a week or more.

Are there ladies at the Leas?

Miss Ingram. She came here to a ball Mr Rochester gave.

What was she like?

Tall, graceful. She was greatly admired for her beauty.

When alone, I looked into my heart. Common sense pronounced, '*You* of importance to him in any way? Cover your face and be ashamed!'

'You have nothing to do with the master of Thornfield.'

dusk closed – evening came
er – Grace Poole

Mr Rochester had been absent for upwards of a fortnight, when the post brought a letter.

Mr Rochester is to return soon?

In three days, and the fine people at the Leas are coming with him.

The party was expected to arrive on Thursday afternoon. I was as active as anybody. I chanced to see Grace Poole and watched her glide along the gallery. All her time was spent in some chamber of the third story.

I once overhead Leah and one of the **charwomen**. Grace formed the subject.

She gets good wages.

She understands what she has to do, and not every one could fill her shoes, not for all the money she gets.

Doesn't she know?

There was a mystery at Thornfield.

charwomen – cleaning women

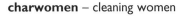

28

Friends return with Mr Rochester. Jane accepts that he will marry someone else.

Thursday afternoon arrived. Adèle flew to the window. I followed; taking care to stand so that I could see without being seen.

Mr Rochester, on his black horse: at his side rode a lady.

Miss Ingram!

Now, while the ladies are in their rooms, I will get you something to eat.

Do you think Mr Rochester will send for us after dinner?

No, I don't.

The next day, Mrs Fairfax was standing at the window with me.

Mr Rochester said, 'Let **her** come in after dinner, and request Miss Eyre to accompany her.'

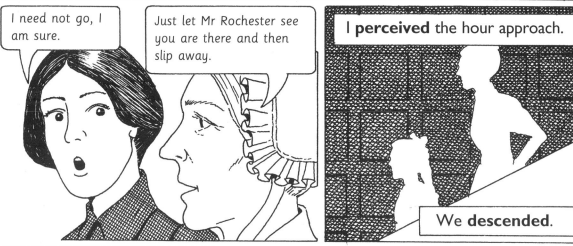

I need not go, I am sure.

Just let Mr Rochester see you are there and then slip away.

I **perceived** the hour approach.

We **descended**.

A band of ladies stood in the opening.

I curtseyed: one or two bent their heads in return; the others only stared at me.

her – Adèle   **perceived** – felt   **descended** – came downstairs

Mr Rochester, without looking at me, began **conversing** with some of the ladies.

My eyes were drawn to his face.

I had not intended to love him.

He made me love him without looking at me.

I made my exit by the side-door.

My sandal was loose; I stopped to tie it.

conversing – talking

Rising, I stood face to face with Mr Rochester.

Why did you not come and speak to me in the room?

I did not wish to disturb you.

What is the matter?

Nothing at all, sir. I am tired.

And a little depressed. What about? Tell me.

Nothing – nothing, sir.

Well, to-night I excuse you; but so long as my visitors stay, I expect you to appear every evening.

Merry days were those at Thornfield Hall. I could not unlove him, because I felt sure he would soon marry Miss Ingram. But I was not jealous: or very rarely.

The arrival of Mr Mason has a very strange effect on Mr Rochester!

One day, **verging on dusk**, a post-chaise stopped and a gentleman **alighted**.

It appears I come when my friend, Mr Rochester, is from home. I think I may **instal myself here** till he returns.

Two or three sat near him, and I caught scraps of their conversation. The new comer was called Mr Mason; I learnt that he was just arrived in England from the West Indies.

Are you aware that a stranger has arrived here since you left?

A stranger! I expected no one.

His name is Mason, sir.

Mason! – the West Indies!

Go into the room up to Mason and whisper in his ear that Mr Rochester is come and wishes to see him: show him in here, and then leave me.

verging on dusk – towards evening
alighted – got out
instal myself here – stay

One night, a terrible event occurs. Jane is worried but receives no answers to her questions.

The moon was full and bright. It was beautiful.

A cry! The night was **rent** by a savage, sharp sound that ran from end to end of Thornfield Hall.

My pulse stopped: my heart stood still.

The cry died. It came out of the third story. I heard a struggle, and a voice shouted – 'Help!'

rent – torn

What has taken place?

A servant has had a nightmare; that is all. Back into your rooms.

I dressed, to be ready for emergencies. A hand tapped at the door.

Are you up?

Yes, sir.

Come out quietly.

Come this way, and make no noise.

He stopped in the corridor of the third story.

Have you a sponge in your room? And **salts**?

Yes.

Go back and fetch both.

I returned.

You don't turn sick at the sight of blood?

He turned the key and opened the door. I heard a snarling sound, laughter.

salts – smelling-salts

Here, Jane!

A man sat, still; his head leant back; his eyes were closed.

I recognized the stranger, Mason. One arm was soaked in blood.

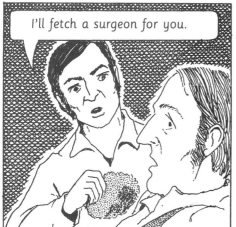

I'll fetch a surgeon for you.

Jane, I shall have to leave you in this room for an hour, perhaps two. You will not speak to him.

The key grated in the lock. I shuddered at the thought of Grace Poole bursting out upon me. And this man — what brought him here? And why, now, was he so tame under the violence done to him?

Presently, Mr Rochester entered, and with him the surgeon.

This wound was not done with a knife: there have been teeth here.

She bit me when Rochester got the knife from her.

I did not expect it: she looked so quiet at first.

I warned you.

She sucked the blood: she said she'd drain my heart.

We shall **get you off cannily**, Dick.

Jane, tell the driver of the post-chaise to be ready.

Take care of him.

get you off cannily – get you away secretly

37

You have passed a strange night, Jane.

Yes, sir.

And it has made you look pale – were you afraid when I left you alone with Mason?

I was afraid of some one coming out of the inner room.

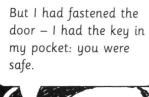

But I had fastened the door – I had the key in my pocket: you were safe.

Will Grace Poole live here still, sir?

Oh yes! Don't trouble your head about her.

It seems to me your life is hardly secure while she stays.

Never fear – I will take care of myself.

Is the danger gone?

I cannot vouch for that till Mason is out of England.

Jane returns to the house of her childhood, where her aunt is dying. She discovers she has an uncle!

On the afternoon of the day following I was summoned down stairs by a message that some one wanted me. A man dressed in deep mourning.

Robert! I remember you. I hope no one is dead.

Mr John.

Missis had a stroke and was pronouncing your name – 'fetch Jane Eyre!'

I went in search of Mr Rochester.

If you please, sir, I want leave of absence for a week or two to see a sick lady – Mrs Reed.

How do you know her?

Mr Reed was my uncle, – my mother's brother.

You said you had no relations.

None that would own me, sir.

Promise me you *will* come back.

I reached Gateshead. Well did I remember Mrs Reed's face: stern and harsh.

Jane Eyre?

Yes, how are you?

Well: I must get it over. Go to my dressing-case, open it, and take out a letter.

I obeyed her directions.

Read it.

Madam,

Will you send me the address of my niece, Jane Eyre. I wish to adopt her and **bequeath** her at my death whatever I may have to leave.

John Eyre,
Madeira.

It was dated three years back.

Why did I never hear of this?

Because I disliked you.

bequeath – give

At twelve o'clock that night she died.

40

On returning to Thornfield, Jane finds out Mr Rochester's true feelings.

I was going back to Thornfield. Mr Rochester had left for London. Mrs Fairfax **surmised** that he was gone to make arrangements for his wedding, as he had talked of purchasing a new carriage.

Mr Rochester

I did not think I should tremble in this way when I saw him.

There you are! Absent from me a whole month: and forgetting me quite, I'll be sworn!

You must see the carriage, Jane, and tell me if you don't think it will suit Mrs Rochester exactly.

A fortnight of calm succeeded my return. There were no visits to Ingram Park. I began to cherish hopes that the match was broken off. Never had I loved him so well.

On Midsummer-eve, I walked a while. Mr Rochester followed me.

surmised – thought

Adèle must go to school; and you, Miss Eyre, must get a new situation.

Yes, sir.

We have been good friends, Jane; have we not?

I sobbed.

I grieve to leave Thornfield: I love Thornfield: — it strikes me with terror to feel I must be torn from you for ever.

I see the necessity of departure.

Where do you see the necessity.

In the shape of Miss Ingram — your bride.

What bride? I have no bride!

But you will have.

Yes — I will! My bride is here. Jane, will you marry me?

Do you truly love me?

I do.

Then, sir, I will marry you.

The wedding is announced. Jane decides to write to the uncle she has never met.

I left my bed in the morning and dressed, wondering if it were a dream.

Good-morning. You look truly pretty this morning.

Gratify my curiosity. Why did you make me believe you wished to marry Miss Ingram?

To render you as madly in love with me as I was with you. Were you jealous?

Never mind. **Communicate your intentions** to Mrs Fairfax, sir.

When I heard Mr Rochester quit Mrs Fairfax's parlour, I hurried down to it. Her eyes expressed surprise.

Can you tell me whether it is actually true that Mr Rochester has asked you to marry him?

Yes.

I hope all will be right in the end, but, be careful.

I remembered the letter of my uncle, John Eyre.

I will write and tell my uncle I am going to be married.

Communicate your intentions – Tell your plan

Jane has a very frightening experience. Mr Rochester's reaction adds to the mystery.

The bridal day; and all preparations for its arrival were complete. Jane Rochester would be born to-morrow, some time after eight o'clock a.m.

Sir, last night I dreamt that Thornfield Hall was a ruin.

On waking, I thought – it is daylight! But it was only candle-light. Sophie, I supposed, had come in.

Then my blood crept cold. This was not Sophie, not Leah, not Mrs Fairfax – not even Grace Poole.

It must have been one of them.

It seemed a woman; tall, with thick and dark hair hanging down her back.

She took my veil and threw it over her own head.

The figure stopped – she thrust her candle close to my face.

Sir, tell me who and what that woman was.

It must have been unreal.

But, sir, this morning when I looked round the room, I saw the veil torn from top to bottom in two halves!

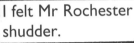

I felt Mr Rochester shudder.

Thank God it was only the veil that was harmed.

That woman must have been Grace Poole.

You ask why I keep such a woman in my house: when we have been married a year and a day, I will tell you; but not now.

And now, no more **sombre** thoughts.

sombre – sad/serious

45

The day of the wedding ... but someone knows a secret and is determined to tell!

Sophie came at seven to dress me.

Jane, are you ready?

There were no bridesmaids, no relatives: none but Mr Rochester and I. I was hurried along by a stride I could hardly follow. We entered the quiet temple.

The service began.

Wilt thou have this woman for thy wedded wife?

The marriage cannot go on: I declare the existence of an **impediment**.

Proceed.

I cannot.

impediment – obstacle

What is the nature of the impediment?

A previous marriage. Mr Rochester has a wife now living.

My name is Briggs — a solicitor.

Edward Rochester married Bertha Mason.

It does not prove my wife is still living.

She is now living at Thornfield Hall. I saw here there. I am her brother.

I never heard of a Mrs Rochester at Thornfield Hall.

No — by God! I took care that none should hear of her.

Close your book: there will be no wedding to-day.

I married fifteen years ago. Bertha Mason is mad — as I found out after I had wed. I invite you all to come up to the house and visit Mrs Poole's patient, *my wife*! You shall see what sort of a being I was cheated into **espousing**.

This girl thought all was fair and legal.

Come, all of you, follow!

espousing – marrying

47

We mounted the staircase to the third story. In a room without a window, Grace Poole bent over the fire. In the deep shade, at the end of the room, a figure ran backwards and forwards.

It snarled and growled like some strange wild animal.

I recognized that face.

The lunatic sprang.

They struggled.

She almost throttled him. He could have settled her with a blow; but he would not strike: he would only wrestle. Grace Poole gave him a **cord**, and he bound her to a chair.

That is *my* wife.

And *this* is what I wished to have: this young girl.

You, madam, are cleared from all blame: your uncle will be glad to hear it.

My uncle! Do you know him?

Mr Mason does. He **implored** Mr Mason to prevent the false marriage.

My hopes were all dead.

cord – rope
implored – begged

Jane tells Mr Rochester that she will leave him and Thornfield.

Some time in the afternoon I passed out. I fell, but I was supported by Mr Rochester.

Jane, I never meant to wound you. Will you ever forgive me?

I forgave him.

You shall yet be my wife. I shall keep only to you so long as I live.

Sir, your wife is living.

Jane, I have for the first time found what I can truly love – I have found *you*.

Mr Rochester, I will *not* be yours.

You are leaving me?

Yes.

That night I departed.

I was out of Thornfield.

After walking for days, Jane is taken in by some kind people in the village of Morton, where they look after her. She is even offered a job!

I walked a long time. The silhouette of a house rose to view.

I groped out the door, and knocked.

What do you want?

A night's shelter and bread to eat.

Let her sit there and ask her no questions.

With the servant's aid, my dripping clothes were removed; soon, a warm, dry bed received me. About three days and nights I lay motionless as a stone.

You *shall* stay here.

The more I knew of the inmates of Moor House, the better I liked them. Days passed like hours, and weeks like days.

Morton had no school. I established one for boys. I mean now to open a second school for girls. I have hired a building for the purpose, with a cottage for the mistress's house. Will you be this mistress?

Thank you. I accept with all my heart.

Jane begins to settle down in her new life at Morton, but the past catches up with her!

The village school opened. I had twenty scholars. It was hard work at first.

Their parents **loaded me with attentions**. I became a favourite in the neighbour-hood. Whenever I went out, I was welcomed with friendly smiles.

It was beginning to snow. The next day I heard a noise: the wind shook the door. St John Rivers came in.

Since yesterday, I have experienced the excitement of a person to whom a tale has been half-told, and is impatient to hear **the sequel**.

I will be the **narrator**, you a listener. The story is short.

He tells her a story – HER life story so far! He also brings her surprising news!

Is it not an odd tale?

Just tell me this – what of Mr Rochester?

loaded ... attentions – made a fuss of me
the sequel – what follows

narrator – storyteller

Briggs wrote to me of a Jane Eyre. You own the name?

Yes.

Briggs wanted to tell you that your uncle is dead; that he has left you all his property, you are now rich.

It puzzles me to know why Mr Briggs wrote to you about me.

Your mother was my father's sister. We are cousins.

Perhaps you think I had forgotten Mr Rochester, reader, amidst these changes of place and fortune. Not for a moment. I had inquired but not a word reached me.

Jane, come to India with me. God intended you for a missionary's wife.

You have been my adopted brother: I, your adopted sister: you and I had better not marry.

You think of Mr Rochester?

I must find out what is become of him.

I announced that I was going on a journey.

Jane sets out to Thornfield to find Mr Rochester. There are shocks and surprises in store!

I left Moor House. It was a journey of six-and-thirty hours.

I looked towards a stately house: I saw a blackened ruin.

Some answer must be had. I could find it nowhere but at the inn.

Is Mr Rochester living at Thornfield Hall now?

No one is living there. It was burnt down about harvest time.

There was a lady – a lunatic, kept in the house. Turned out to be Mr Rochester's wife!

She set fire to the **hangings** of her room.

Then she made her way to the chamber that had been the governess's.

hangings – curtains

Mr Rochester?

He got the servants out and went back to get his mad wife.

She was on the roof. We saw him approach her.

She yelled, gave a spring, and lay smashed on the pavement. Dead.

He was alive?

Yes, but he is blind.

He was taken out from the ruins, alive, but one eye was knocked out, and one hand so crushed the surgeon had to **amputate it**. The other eye inflamed: he lost the sight of that also.

Where is he?

At Ferndean, thirty miles off.

If your boy can drive me to Ferndean before dark, I'll pay twice the hire you usually demand.

amputate it – cut it off

Jane and Mr Rochester are reunited. They still love each other and a decision is made.

The manor-house of Ferndean was deep buried in a wood. It was as still as a church. I drew near and knocked.

Tell your master that a person wishes to speak to him, but do not give my name.

She returned.

You are to send in your name.

Give the tray to me, I will carry it in.

I approached him.

I am here. I came this evening.

Who is it? Is it Jane?

I am come back to you.

I am an independent woman now. My uncle is dead, and he left me five thousand pounds.

And will you stay with me?

Unless you object. I will be your nurse, your housekeeper, your companion.

You cannot always be my nurse — you must marry one day.

I thought you would be revolted, Jane, when you saw my arm, and my **visage**.

Am I hideous, Jane?

Very, sir: you always were, you know.

I began the **narrative** of my experience for the last year. Of course, St John Rivers's name came in.

You have formed a new tie. Go — with the husband you have chosen — this St John Rivers.

My heart is yours, sir: it belongs to you.

Will you marry me? A poor blind, crippled man?

visage – face   **narrative** – story

At last they are married. Good things begin to happen and their life together is one of happiness.

Reader, I married him.

When we got back from church, I went into the kitchen.

Mary, I have married Mr Rochester this morning.

I seed you go out with the master, but I didn't know you were gone to be wed.

He's done right. I wish you joy, Miss.

Thank you.

I wrote to Moor House to say what I had done.

Diana approved. How St John received the news I don't know; he never answered the letter: yet, six months after he wrote to me. His letter was calm and kind. He hopes I am happy.

And little Adèle?

I took care she should never want for anything.

I have now been married ten years.

Mr Rochester continued blind for the first two years of our **union**. One morning, he came and bent over me.

Jane, have you a glittering ornament round your neck? And a pale blue dress on?

He and I went up to London. He had the advice of an **eminent oculist**; and he eventually recovered the sight of that one eye. He cannot see very distinctly; but he can find his way without being led.

When his first-born was put into his arms, he could see that the boy had inherited his own eyes, as they once were. My Edward and I, then, are happy.

The End

union – marriage   **eminent oculist** – famous eye doctor